By the residents of Eleonas Camp, Athens, Greece.

RECIPES
WELCOME

project elea

Refugee: a person who has been forced to leave their country in order to escape war, persecution or natural disaster.

Mediterranean Sea
2015-2018

Arrivals: 1,649,993
Dead or missing: 12,364

_____

Every 2 seconds, 1 person is forcibly displaced as a result of conflict or persecution.

_____

In 2018, 2 out of every 100 people who attempted to cross the Mediterranean Sea died.

#safepassage

Source: UNHCR

For those, who by trying to secure the lives of loved ones

have given everything, including their own.

Title: RECIPES WELCOME. THE REFUGEE RECIPES THAT BORDERS COULD'T STOP
ISBN 978-618-84101-3-8

Original idea and direction: Francisco Gentico.
Design and typesetting: Simone Plassard.
Food stylist: Maria Angeles Torres.
Cover design: Simone Plassard and Francisco Gentico.
Copy Editing: Lucy Peploe.

© Photography
Maria Angeles Torres pages 15, 17, 19, 23, 29, 33, 37, 41, 45, 49, 51, 53, 57, 59, 63, 67, 69, 71, 73, 75, 77, 81, 85, 91, 93, 97 and 98.
Francisco Gentico pages 12, 14, 16, 20, 21, 22, 24, 25, 26, 30, 31, 32, 35, 36, 38, 39, 40, 42, 44, 47, 48, 50, 52, 56, 58, 60, 62, 64, 65, 66, 68, 70, 72, 74, 76, 80, 82, 83, 84, 87, 88, 89, 90, 92, 94, 95 and cover.
Natalia Navarro pages 46 and 86.
Rebekah Cheng page 28.
Sergi Camara pages 2, 3 and 4.
Brad Fredricks pages 54 and 78.

Originally printed in December 2018.

ISBN 978-618-84101-3-8

www.projectelea.org

CONTENTS

All proceeds from this cookbook will benefit Project Elea
and the residents of Eleonas Refugee Camp.

PROLOGUE

When I was in elementary school back in New York City, students were required to study different nations of the world: Mexico, France, China, Egypt. Since this was in the days before the Internet, however, we were mostly expected to learn about these countries through textbooks. These books offered such riveting insights as: "Swahili is one of several native languages of Kenya," "A primary export of Greece is olive oil," and "winter comes early to the Ural mountains."

But my teacher was smart.

Instead, she had us eat.

As Americans, everyone in my class was descended from other nationalities. Our teacher assigned us to bring in recipes from our "countries of origin" to compile into an international cookbook. One boy brought in a recipe for enchiladas. A girl brought in a recipe for shumi dumplings. Another brought in a sample of Welsh rarebit. Marzipan. Borscht. Stuffed vine leaves. Chicken teriyaki. By learning about these foods, we learned about other nations' agriculture, history, and lifestyles. Then, in the school's tiny kitchen, we prepared these foods together one afternoon and ate a "global lunch." Each time my classmates and I tasted something we'd never eaten before, a whole new world opened on our tongues.

Food is many things. Above all, of course, it is sustenance: the way all of us stay alive. It is also the most fundamental form of love. The very first act a parent ever does is to feed their new baby. But food is also culture. And art. And, perhaps above all, language. It's the way we communicate with each other -- particularly when we don't have words in common. The easiest gateway we have into strangers' cultures and hearts is through food. By sitting down together, sharing a meal, and sampling each other's cuisine, we become more intimate, more curious, more knowing.

American chef and commentator Anthony Bourdain has said: "Food is everything we are. It's an extension of nationalist feeling, ethnic feeling, your personal history, your province, your region, your tribe, your grandma." And sometimes, when we have to flee our homelands, our cuisines are all we can take with us. Recipes are portable the way few other things in a culture are. You may have to leave Kabul, or Aleppo, or Warsaw, or Dakar, or Limerick, or Misrata, or Da Nang, or Sarajevo with only the clothes on your back. But you will also carry your knowledge of your cooking with you.

Right now, the residents at the Eleonas Refugee Camp in Athens, Greece hail from more than twenty-six nations around the world. None of them, of course, ever planned on becoming refugees. Before they left their native countries, they were people with homes, families, lives, jobs, and dreams. Now, their cuisine is often all they have left of their culture.

For those of us who have volunteered at Eleonas, the residents' hospitality is continually overwhelming. They are always inviting us to eat with them. Using meager camp allowances, they purchase ingredients that they transform on hotplates into extraordinary meals. In doing so, they transform all of us as well.

When we all eat together, we are no longer "refugees" and "volunteer workers," but "hosts" and "guests." We are equalized and normalized for a few minutes in the midst of a horrific geopolitical situation. We sit together and chew and swallow and laugh. The best of ourselves comes forth with stews and rice and curries and bread.

Too often, the world sees "refugees" as a faceless, suffering, threatening mass. By telling the stories of the cooks here, we hope to remind the world-at-large that the people it often fears are complex and beautiful human beings with rich histories and talents. They're people with family recipes, with a love of food, who will stand over a small pot, smiling as they stir in coriander and salt. They are women who take pride in making pickles and bread, in chopping tomatoes and preparing jeweled rice. They are, in short, like our parents, like "grandma." They are, in fact, us.

Susan Jane Gilman, bestselling author and Project Elea volunteer.

salads and sides

RIZ AU GRAS

BIBA
GUINEA

SERVES
8

PREP.
10 MIN

COOK
20 MIN

Nobody taught me how to cook. When I was 16 I lived near a military camp. My friends and I would see the soldiers coming back from the market with food and watch them cook. I would also watch my mum cooking, and I liked learning from her, but I never cooked with her. In Guinea I studied mechanics.

I left Guinea more than two years ago through Senegal, Morocco and Turkey. After that I went to Kos by boat. It was a small boat with 46 people. On the way it started raining heavily and the engine stopped. The boat was rocking a lot and people started falling, 15 of them, including my best friend. We lost them. A woman from Iraq fell into the water, she was holding onto my leg and I tried to help her hang on but I couldn't anymore, if I had, I would have fallen too. Eventually she couldn't hold herself anymore and she drowned. To this day, when I go to the beach and into the sea, I remember this moment and I stop myself from going in too deep.

This dish is most often cooked by Guinean women although there are few men who know how to cook it. I was about 19 when I learnt it. One night, I said to my mum - "Tonight, I will cook the meal" and she said, "But you don't know how, nobody has taught you!" I told her not to worry and that I would do it. Later I called my mum and dad to come and eat. They were shocked and they said, "did somebody outside teach you?"

I like cooking, but not alone. Even when I'm outside of the camp and I'm really hungry, I wait until I get home to cook. I need someone, anyone, to cook and eat with me. In Eleonas I first lived with five other people from Guinea, Mali, Senegal and Uganda. We used to put our money together and cook and eat together which was really nice. Unfortunately this tradition died out when some of them moved on.

INGREDIENTS

6 onions
4 cloves of garlic
4 large tomatoes
4 bell peppers (green preferably)
4 stock cubes (chicken or vegetable)
125ml/4fl oz vegetable oil
2 tsp salt
2 tsp black pepper
1 1/2 tsp hot chili pepper
1kg/2lb white rice

STEPS

1 Peel the onions and wash all the vegetables. Dice the onions, peppers and tomatoes.

2 Pour the oil into a saucepan and, when it is hot, add the diced vegetables. Stir everything well and then reduce the heat, put on a lid and let the vegetables cook for about 8 minutes.

3 Add 4 large glasses of water, along with the salt and stock cubes. Stir well. Put in the black pepper and finely chopped garlic. Mix everything together and simmer fot 5 to 10 minutes. Taste and season with salt if required.

4 Finally, add the rice, stir well, adding more water if needed. Let it cook until the water has been absorbed by the rice, stirring once in a while.

Eat with chicken, fish or alone.

SALATA ASWAD

MUSTAFA
SUDAN

SERVES
8

PREP.
20 MIN

COOK
1 HR

I learned how to cook from my mother. Every time she cooked, I watched, helping when I could, and I learned quickly. Cooking means a lot of things to me. Some days I dream about being a professional cook. Cooking means possibilities. I like many types of food from all nationalities, so I can keep trying all different kinds of recipes all the time.

Living in Sudan was a little bad, but not too bad. Then the war made it bad. I do love my country and how my life used to be. I was studying before, and I hope that since I have moved away, I can return to studying. When I left I travelled from Sudan to Egypt and then to Turkey. It took a total of one year. From Turkey I took a boat to Chios which was an extremely difficult time.

My life is better in Athens, but not by that much. It is better to live with people that don't fight, but at the same time they still make problems. It seems to be a recurring problem, but life without war is definitely better.

In the future I want to be the President of Sudan. I definitely want to finish studying and live in England, the USA, or even Canada for some time.

INGREDIENTS

2 aubergines/eggplants
425g/14oz red kidney beans, canned
1 tbsp peanut butter, crunchy
1 tsp salt
1 tsp pepper
1 clove garlic, crushed

STEPS

1 Peel and dice the eggplants.

2 Heat oil in a pan with the salt, pepper, and crushed garlic. To the pan add the eggplant and fry until soft (20-25 minutes).

3 Drain and mash the can of red kidney beans. Stir into the eggplant along with 1tbsp of peanut butter.

Serve with pita bread.

TABBOULEH

REJA
SYRIA

SERVES
8

PREP.
45 MIN

COOK
0 MIN

I am from Damascus, Syria. I got married when I was 14 and had two kids at 16. I learned to cook while visiting my sisters and watching how they cooked and trying it when I went home. I also like to discover new things and ways to cook by myself. I like to prepare the food. Cooking makes me happy and fills me with joy. While cooking I become focused because I want to make a good dish and I like to add my own touch to my food.

My life was very difficult in Damascus because of the war. I moved around to different places and houses to try to stay safe. Finally I walked for one and a half months from Syria to Turkey. Then I travelled from Turkey to Mitilini by boat before coming to Athens. My son went to Germany before me and I tried to follow him, but now the borders are closed and it is more difficult to get to Germany.

The first time I stepped foot into Athens, I felt safe. I am not looking back but looking forward to my new life. Even though I am tired, sick, and constantly waiting, I don't care because I have a goal and that is to see my son again *[Reja is now in Germany with her son]*.

INGREDIENTS

5 tomatoes, diced
3 cucumbers, diced
250g/8oz fine ground bulgar wheat
5 bunches fresh parsley
1 large onion, finely chopped
juice of 3-4 lemons
4 sprigs fresh mint leaves, finely chopped
175ml/6fl oz olive oil
1 tsp salt
1/4 tsp freshly ground black pepper
romaine lettuce leaves, for serving (optional)

STEPS

1 Put the bulgar wheat into a bowl and cover with warm water. Soak until softened, about 20 minutes. Drain the bulgur in a fine mesh sieve, pressing with the back of a spoon to extract the excess water. Fluff the bulgur with a fork.

2 Wash the parsley, allow it to dry, and slice into thin strips. Finely cut the mint.

3 Chop the tomatoes, cucumbers and onion. Combine with the parsley, mint and bulgar in a large bowl.

4 In a separate bowl whisk together the lemon juice, olive oil, salt and pepper. Gently combine the dressing mixture with the bulgar and salad.

Serve the Tabbouleh with lettuce leaves to use as a scoop to eat.

VEGETARIAN KIBBEH

HIBA
SYRIA

SERVES
5

PREP.
2 HRS

COOK
0 MIN

My family and I are from Aleppo but moved to Damascus for work. They taught me how to cook. I enjoy cooking and adding my own touch to food. My husband and I baked bread for our neighbours in Syria and continue to do so in camp. Cooking brings families together. We like to eat special meals together.

Before the war our life was very good but after the war things got very bad. We lived in Raqqa where there were a lot of Daesh, and I would always have people tell me that I needed to have my face covered. We saw horrible things on the streets of our city.

From Raqqa we went illegally to Turkey and were there for two and a half months. It was very difficult there because everything was very expensive. We went to Izmir and then to Mitilini, Greece. We stayed there for two and a half months and then got moved to Athens because I was pregnant. We are fine here. Not very happy or very sad. Here in Greece we don't hear fighter planes or wake up to people dying in front of us so it's better than in Syria but here we do not have enough money.

I would like to be a chef someday and I want to be with my mom in Germany.

INGREDIENTS

2 large onions
500g/1lb spicy red peppers, seeds removed
4 medium tomatoes
1kg/2lb fine ground bulgur wheat
3 tsp salt
1 tsp red chili powder
1 tsp ground cumin
3 tbsp olive oil

To garnish:
a few lettuce leaves
2 lemons
1/2 cucumber
a small bunch of parsley
olive oil

STEPS

1
Soak the bulgur wheat in water for 1½hours. Then drain and put into a food processor. Add the finely chopped onions, red peppers and tomatoes.

2
Blend until quite smooth but not pureed. Transfer to a bowl and add the salt, cumin and red chili powder (to taste) and mix well.

3
Pour in the olive oil and combine until the mixture has a moldable consistency, adding more oil as required. Use your hands to roll into log-shaped patties and garnish with lettuce, cucumber, parsley and slices of lemon.

4
Drizzle with olive oil.

CHEESE BALLS

AISHA
PALESTINE

SERVES
6

PREP.
3 HRS

COOK
30 MIN

I make Palestinian, Lebanese or I can say Middle Eastern food. This recipe is a variation of manaqish which is foldable dough topped with different things like Zaater, cheese, meat or kishik and it is famous in Palestine, Lebanon, Syria and Jordan. I burnt a lot of dishes while trying to cook, but later I learned with the help of my older sister and people from the camp in Lebanon who have cooking experience. When I went to university in Lebanon I took elective courses about cooking, arts and cost control to add more practical skills than just a degree on paper.

Cooking is enjoyment, food is love. The kitchen is a place for learning deeply about my culture and to start to find connections with other cultures around me. Sometimes I find it interesting to open discussion about the roots of some dishes from history.

In the camp in Lebanon, with a group of artists, I founded the Palestinian Space Agency. It was a virtual agency online making a political statement about freedom of movement for Palestinians; 'when you have nowhere to go, go to space'. We received a lot of CV's and emails from people thinking we were an actual space agency. Because of this I became the point of contact for the Space Generation Advisory Council. We even created Arabic food that could be eaten in space.

When I was 17, I also created a creative studio space in the camp. At the beginning it was for music but then I moved into experimental movies. Here in Eleonas I run movie workshops to teach other residents to make short movies. I love Athens. I feel like I knew it before but somehow I've been lost to where I can begin to build my life and/or find myself.

INGREDIENTS

500g/1lb white flour
7g/1/4oz yeast
1 tsp baking powder
1 tsp salt
250ml/8fl oz milk
250ml/8fl oz water
5 drops vanilla extract
125ml/4fl oz olive oil
1 medium size egg
30g nigella sativa (can use black cumin)
450g salted cheese (like akawi/feta)
2 tbsp fresh thyme
2 tbsp fresh oregano
2 tbsp fresh basil
3 tbsp olive oil

STEPS

1 Mix the flour, yeast, baking powder and salt together in a large mixing bowl. Stir in the olive oil, milk and vanilla extract. Gradually add the water, mixing well to form a soft dough.

2 Turn the dough out onto a floured work surface and knead for about five minutes, until smooth and elastic. Transfer to a clean bowl and leave to rise for about 3 hours or until doubled in size.

3 Break the cheese into small pieces using a fork. Mix in the fresh herbs and olive oil.

4 Pre-heat the oven to 180°C/350°F. Shape the rested dough into small balls. Push a generous amount of the cheese mix into the centre of each ball. Pinch the dough to seal in the cheese and arrange on an oven tray.

5 Lightly whisk an egg and use a brush to coat each ball. Sprinkle nigella sativa onto the balls. Allow balls to rest for another 5-10 minutes. Cook in the oven for approximately 20-30minutes, until golden brown.

FATIR NAAN

MINA
AFGHANISTAN

SERVES
4

PREP.
1 HR

COOK
30 MIN

When I was a kid, I used to enjoy watching the women of my family cooking and my mother-in-law taught me how. I have always loved to cook. For me it is a way to show love. That's why, when someone comes to my home, I like to cook for them.

The situation in my country at the beginning was good, but when the Taliban came, everything changed and it was not good. Everything was very violent. Women were not allowed to work or go outside by themselves. That's why we left the country. We tried 3 times to cross into Turkey but they deported us back.

We came to Greece by boat. On the journey we met a family that had a daughter the same age as mine. After we arrived in Chios my family spent some days in a camp there until moving to Athens and Eleonas. One night we went to sleep and a new family was moved into the next room of our container. In the morning we found out that it was the family from the boat! It is nice. It is like we knew them from the beginning, like parallel lives.

I like our life in the camp, especially for my daughter who has many friends here now, but in the future I want to go to Germany so my small daughter can go to school, we can learn the language and cook for the rest of our lives,

INGREDIENTS

175g/6oz all-purpose flour
250ml/8fl oz milk
125ml/4fl oz oil
1 tbsp yeast
1/2 tbsp salt

STEPS

1 In a bowl mix together the dry ingredients (flour, yeast and salt). Make a well in the mixture and pour in around half of the oil and milk.

2 Begin to fold in the liquid and knead the mixture. Add the remaining milk and oil small amounts at a time to form a smooth dough texture. Move the dough to a floured surface and knead, adding more milk or flour if necessary, The dough should be soft but not sticky.

3 Allow the dough to rest for 30 minutes or an hour (until doubled in size). Preheat oven to 240°C/475°F. Roll the dough out into one round piece, about 2cm (just under an inch) in thickness. Place it on a lightly oiled baking tray.

4 Cook for 30 minutes or until golden brown.

poultry

CHICKEN BIRYANI

KANWAL
PAKISTAN

SERVES
8

PREP.
30 MIN

COOK
1 HR

My mother taught me to cook when I was 13. I enjoy cooking because I like to eat and I want to make new things. Cooking is very necessary because if you are not a good cook your husband can beat you and your in-laws get angry.

My life in Pakistan was excellent. We had lots of money, a business, a house, everything. I miss my bedroom. We came to Greece because we are Shia Muslims. Sipah-e-Sahaba (a group that works with Al Qaeda in Afghanistan) threatened my husband. In 2012, they burned down his clothes shop.

We travelled from Pakistan to Iran and then walked from Iran to Turkey. I was pregnant when we left. We were kidnapped by Kurds at the border in the mountains and they stole money and jewellery. There were five days where we did not eat. I thought my daughter was dead. I had to check if she was breathing. We fed her melted snow. The first two times we tried to cross into Turkey, the police caught us and sent us back. After the second time we met a man who said we could stay at his house. They gave us food and room. When we woke up, they came back with knives and said they were going to cut our throats unless we gave them everything. We gave away the rest of our money, mobiles and jewellery, but he said they needed more. We contacted my mother and she sent us more. That is when they finally released us.

After we crossed the border we took a boat to Lesvos. My daughter Abiha was dehydrated, so we stayed in the hospital for 5-6 days before moving to Athens. Life here is not better than Pakistan, but it is okay and at least we are safe.

INGREDIENTS

1.5kg/3lbs basmati rice
4-5 medium onions, sliced
4-5 tomatoes, diced
1.5kg/3lb chicken breast
2 tsp garlic paste
2 tsp ginger paste
350ml/12fl oz cooking oil
50g/1.75oz Masaledar
Sindhi Biryani Masala
Spice Mix*
3-4 tbsp plain yogurt
Optional: ½ tbsp yellow
food coloring
Optional yogurt sauce:
1 cup yogurt
12-13 leaves of mint
8 green chili peppers,
seeds removed and diced
1/2 tsp salt

*See index page. 96

STEPS

1 Wash the basmati rice, then boil until cooked (approx. 12 minutes). In a separate pan, fry the onions in the oil until light brown. Add the diced chicken and fry for 10 minutes.

2 Add the Spice Mix. Once the spices are sizzling, add the garlic and ginger pastes. Stir them with the chicken, spices and onions until aromatic. Then, add the yogurt, mix well and cook for a further 5 minutes. Add the tomatoes and continue to cook until soft.

3 In a deep pot or saucepan, layer the cooked rice and chicken mixture until finished (3 or 4 layers of each). Cover with a lid and cook on a low heat on top of the stove for 5-10 minutes. *If desired, food coloring can be added at this stage.* Before serving, mix the rice and chicken together.

4 To prepare the optional sauce:
Put the mint and chili pepper into a blender or food processor and blend finely. Mix with the yogurt and salt.

Serve with yogurt, mango pickle and/or the optional sauce.

MAQLUBA

ZARIFA
SYRIA (KURDISH)

SERVES
8

PREP.
30 MIN

COOK
45 MIN

My mother taught me how to cook when I was 17 years old. The first dish I learned how to cook was chicken with vegetables. We are Kurdish and our city, Aleppo, is all about food. While we are having breakfast we are thinking about what we are going to eat at lunch and dinner.

My life in Aleppo was really comfortable, my husband had a clothes factory and we had everything there. While my husband was working I was taking care of our 3 kids. Everything was perfect before the war started and then we lost everything. We had to leave Syria and we finished by getting to Chios, an island in Greece, by boat. There we lived in a tent for more than a year. Life in that camp was like life in (wartime) Syria. The neo-Nazi groups were attacking the camp every now and then with Molotov bombs.

Now we are in Athens, in Eleonas camp. Life in Greece is hard because there is no work and no opportunities. We want to go somewhere, anywhere in Europe where we could work and make a life for ourselves. We just want a good future for our kids, a place where they can grow up safely.

INGREDIENTS

175g/6oz basmati rice
1kg chicken breast
3 medium potatoes
3 aubergines/eggplants
1 onion
2 chicken stock cubes
walnuts
olive oil
sunflower oil
1 tsp butter
salt
pepper

STEPS

1 Peel the onion and put in a pan with the chicken and salt. Cover with water and boil for approximately 30 minutes. Remove the chicken and let it cool slightly before removing the skin. Cut the chicken into bite-sized pieces.

2 Peel and slice the potatoes and aubergines. Fry them in a generous amount of sunflower oil. In a deep saucepan or cooking pot, melt the butter with the olive oil at a high temperature, then reduce the heat and add the chicken. On top, layer the slices of potato and aubergine.

3 Add rice (washed) as the final layer and sprinkle salt, pepper and the stock cubes (crumbled) on top. Pour 1.5l/48fl oz hot water into the pot and reduce to a medium temperature. Don't stir. When the water has evaporated the dish is ready, approximately 25-30 minutes.

4 In a separate pan stir fry the walnuts in a bit of olive oil. To serve, flip the contents of the pan onto a plate. In Arabic Maqluba is the act of flipping which is where the name of the dish comes from. Add the nuts on top to decorate.

NATJI

SÉKOU
MALI

SERVES
8

PREP.
15 MIN

COOK
50 MIN

I learned to cook at home by watching how my parents cooked. For me food is a way of sharing. You never cook for yourself; you always cook for others, to eat with family and friends.

In Mali things were good, but coming to Europe was a good way to improve my general situation, find a job and have a better life.
To come to Greece I had to go first to Turkey, from there to the islands and then to Athens, where I have lived for more than 2 years.
In Greece my life is good. I spend time with friends, I watch movies, I play football every afternoon, but my life in Mali was better. I didn't know anyone who had come to Europe before. I imagined it as a different place.

I would like to find a job. In Greece it is very difficult and even more for us because of the language. I would love to be able to study, work and have a family.

INGREDIENTS

1/2 chicken (cuts of choice)
6 onions, finely chopped
4 cloves of garlic, finely chopped
4 large tomatoes, finely chopped
4 peppers (green preferably), finely chopped
4 medium potatoes, diced
4 chicken stock cubes
250ml/8fl oz cooking oil
2 tsp salt
2 tsp black pepper
1 1/2 tsp hot chili powder

STEPS

1
Finely chop the onions, tomatoes and peppers. Peel and dice the potatoes. In a pot begin to fry the onions tomatoes and peppers in oil, over high heat. Stir well and cover with a lid. Allow to cook for around 8 minutes. To the pot add 11/32 fl oz of water as well as the salt and stock cubes. Stir well. Add the potatoes, cover and cook for a further 10 minutes.

2
Wash the chicken. Add to the pot and cook for 5-10 minutes. Add the black pepper and garlic. Stir well and leave for 5-10 minutes. Taste and season with salt if needed.

3
When the potatoes are cooked through, remove half of them and mash. Put the mashed potatoes back in the pot and stir. Leave for 5 minutes and then add the hot chili powder.

4
Finally reduce the temperature to a low heat for about 5 minutes before turning off completely.

32

Serve with rice.

CHICKEN KABSA

NAME WITHHELD
SYRIA

SERVES
6

PREP.
30 MIN

COOK
2 HRS

My sister is a very good cook. She taught me how to cook Kabsa. She is five years older than me. She taught me when I was 30 and studying computers at university; before that I did not like cooking. I have five sisters and three brothers, so I always asked my sisters or my mother to cook. I did not want to cook but now I enjoy cooking. Syrian food is very beautiful. In Syria, you cook with a beautiful smile. When I cook I think about Syria. Syrian people like good food.

When you cook you must wear a hijab so you don't get hair in the food. My husband and brothers would be angry if that ever happened.
I came to Athens over 1 year ago. After I left Syria I was in Istanbul for two years; one year with my husband and children, and the following year my husband went to Germany. I was in Chios with my children for 20 days before Athens. In Chios there were many problems. Some Afghans killed two Iraqis, one man and one woman, so my husband paid for a ship to take us to Athens.

Athens is a beautiful city but it isn't as good as Germany. In Germany you get more support. But it is okay here, not the same as Turkey. Turkey doesn't help at all. My husband has a passport in Germany and lives there. I'm worried maybe my husband will find a new wife.

INGREDIENTS

1.5kg/3lb raw chicken
5 cardamom pods
4-5 bay leaves
1 red onion quartered
500g/1lb basmati rice
2 red onions, finely chopped
8 small green chili peppers, seeds removed, finely diced
4 tomatoes, finely diced
2 tbsp chili powder
2 tbsp salt (one for the rice as it is soaking, one for the sauce with chicken)
1/2 tbsp black pepper
1/2 tbsp biharat*
3 tbsp sunflower oil

Optional to serve:
salad (lettuce, cucumber, tomato, onion)
yogurt
pita bread

*See index page. 96

STEPS

1

Clean the chicken and separate into large pieces (drumsticks, wings, breasts, etc). Take one onion and make 4 slits in it but keeping it whole. Fill a large saucepan with water and salt and bring to the boil. Add the bay leaves, cardamom pods, onion and chicken joints.

After 40-50 minutes skim out any fat, cover and continue to boil for a further 20-40 minutes. Total cooking time should be approximately 1.5 hours from frozen or 1 hour from fresh. After cooking, remove the onion and toss.

2

While the chicken is cooking:
Add the rice and salt to 1.8l/3pints of water and soak for 30 minutes. Heat the oil in a large non-stick frying pan over a medium/high heat. Sauté the onion, then add the peppers and tomatoes and cook until soft.

3

Add the sautéed vegetables, salt, chili powder, black pepper and biharat spices directly to the pot of chicken and stir.
Wash the rice 2-3 times until the water runs clear, and then drain.
Remove the chicken cuts (ready to serve) from the sauce and add the drained rice to the pot instead. Turn off the heat and allow the rice to cook in the sauce for 10-12 minutes, using a lid and dish towel to retain heat.

Serve with salad, natural yogurt and/or pita bread.

GORASA BEDAMA

WALID
SUDAN

SERVES
4

PREP.
1 HR

COOK
30 MIN

I learned to cook 10 years ago when I was 18. My mother taught me one day and that was the beginning of everything. After that I learned by myself.

My life in Sudan was normal. I studied to be an engineer there. I had some issues with the government and I left to get a better life. When I was 26 I went to Turkey and there I met my wife who is from Syria. Now we have 2 kids. From Turkey we went to the island of Samos and there we had our first son. My second son was born when we were living at Eleonas camp.

Life in Greece is difficult. I keep trying to study even though there is no work in this country. It is really hard to move forward without options but we try. I would like to learn even more about IT and about mechanical engineering.

I would like to move to Germany or the UK with my wife and kids. In those countries I can develop myself, enhance my knowledge and give my family a good environment to grow.

INGREDIENTS

60ml/2fl oz vegetable oil
4 small onions, diced
1/2kg chicken, diced (cuts of your choice)
1 tsp ground cumin
1 tsp ground coriander
1/4 tsp cinnamon
4-5 tbsp tomato paste
1/4 tbsp salt
5 cloves garlic, crushed
Optional: 1-2 small green chili peppers, finely diced

Bread
750g/24oz flour
1/2 tsp yeast
1/4 tsp salt

STEPS

1
In a large saucepan, heat the oil and fry the onions until the turn a golden colour. Add the chicken and enough water to cover. Bring to the boil, then add the cumin, coriander, cinnamon, tomato paste, salt and chili peppers. Cover and leave to simmer for approximately 20 minutes.

2
Meanwhile, begin preparing the bread. Put the flour, yeast, salt and approximately 500ml/17fl oz of water in a large bowl. Mix together, using your hands and then leave the dough in the bowl to rise. If you have time, let the dough sit for an hour. If not, 20 minutes is fine as well.

3
Using a slotted spoon, remove the spicy chicken and onions from the sauce and place in a serving dish. Add the garlic to the sauce that is left in the pan and mix. Simmer for a further 10 minutes. To cook the bread, heat a frying pan, add some oil and pour in enough dough to make a 0.5cm layer. Cook 1-2 minutes on each side. Repeat until you have cooked all the bread.

4
Serve in three layers:
Bottom layer: Bread spread with sauce.
Middle layer: Bread covered with spicy chicken and onions.
Top layer: Bread.

Eat with your hands, using the bread to sandwich the sauce and meat in each bite. Serve with a salad.

QABELEY

MOHAMMAD
AFGHANISTAN

SERVES
7

PREP.
20 MIN

COOK
1.5 HRS

I like cooking everything - cookies, yoghurt, pickling vegetables - everything. Once I made the best kebab in the world! The thing I really enjoy is cooking for other people and making food for parties. My wife is also a very good cook, but maybe I am better! I love the feeling of cooking and everything about it. When I make food, I want people to come, enjoy and eat. Cooking for myself is not the same. Qabeley is a traditional dish of Afghanistan, but it is known in other places too, and eaten a lot, for example, in Uzbekistan. I buy the ingredients in the Bazaar every weekend.

No one taught me how to cook, I taught myself. I left home alone when I was 13 and went first to Pakistan for a month and then to Iran after that. I stayed in Iran for the next 29 years where I had a big 24hr supermarket, which is still there. When I was 18, I married an Afghani girl and we now have four children, two girls and two boys, who are living in Germany with my wife.

My parents were farmers and they stayed in Afghanistan. I had a problem with my uncle as a boy, which made me fear for my life, so I left. I went to our family in Pakistan, but my uncle told someone there of our feud and they threatened to kill me. I have six brothers and five sisters, but I am the oldest of my siblings. As a young man I worked as a farmer and in the wells. It was when I left home at 13 that I started to cook.

INGREDIENTS

3 large chicken legs, cut in halves or thirds
3 white onions, grated
4 cloves garlic, grated
1 tsp ground pepper
1 tsp turmeric
1½kg/3lb basmati rice
6 medium carrots
125g/4oz currants
125ml/4fl oz sunflower oil
salt

STEPS

1 Put the chicken in a saucepan, cover with water and bring to the boil. Add the onions, garlic, pepper, tumeric and 1 tbsp salt. Reduce the heat and leave to cook for around 30 minutes, stirring occasionally to keep it from sticking. Meanwhile, wash the rice in warm water and rinse. Place in a bowl and add 2 tsp salt and a kettle-full of boiling water. Leave to one side.

2 Prepare the carrots by washing them and then cutting them into thin short strips. Place the currents in a bowl of water to soak.

3 Once the chicken is cooked, make sure the onions and garlic have become almost a puree, by squashing them into the sauce until no longer visible. You will be left with a sort of gravy. Then add 1/2 cup of oil and stir. Remove the meat and gravy from the pan and put to one side in a dish.

4 To a large pan, add 1/4 cup of oil and once hot, add the carrots and 1 tbsp salt. Fry for 20 minutes, stirring regularly. Drain the rice and add to the pan, followed by the currants and a cup of water.

5 Finally, add the cooked chicken and gravy to the rice and carrots along with 1/4 cup of water. Taste, and add more salt if needed. Place a lid on the pan and leave to simmer for 30-45 minutes, over a medium heat. Do not stir.

Serve with yogurt, pickled vegetables and bread.

ZERESHK POLO MORGH

FARAH
IRAN

SERVES
4

PREP.
15 MIN

COOK
1 HR

I learned to cook at home in Tehran when I was 12. My mother taught me. She worked in a shop, so I had to make the meals when she was gone. The first dish I learned to cook was a dish called "Baghi Palou" with onions and chicken that you eat with rice. I was first married at 16, so it was good I knew how to cook. Now, I cook every day. Sometimes, I use a cookbook, but mostly, I know it by heart.

Back in Iran, my husband was a mobile phone technician and I was a childcare provider. I love babies! I didn't want to leave, but I had to because my son and husband were in danger there. We took a bus from Tehran to Turkey; it took two days, and it was so hot. From Izmir, we took a boat to Lesvos, Greece. We were 70 people packed into a small shipping container, all locked in together, squeezed in so tight we couldn't breath or move. It took five hours to cross, and we were very scared. When we finally arrived in Lesvos, my back was so bad (from sitting curled up in the container) that I couldn't walk for two or three days. The Greek police had to put me in a wheelchair.

Now, here in Greece, we actually have received Greek I.D's and passports. Our trouble is, we don't have jobs yet. There are not enough subsidies for us to move out of the camp. I'd like to live in a good neighborhood in Athens. I'd love to be a hairdresser or open a restaurant, but because of my back problem now, I can't walk a lot. If I am safe and healthy, I'd do big things. I do love to cook. But my favorite food of all? Dark chocolate!

INGREDIENTS

2 medium onions, finely chopped
4 chicken joints
1 tsp turmeric
2 tbsp tomato paste
1kg/2lb basmati rice
60g/2oz barberries (or goji berries)
1 tsp saffron
olive oil
pepper
salt
sugar

STEPS

1
Fry the onions in olive oil on medium heat. When golden add the chicken and cook on all sides to seal it. When the skin of the chicken becomes golden add the pepper, salt and turmeric. Stir well and add the tomato paste. Stir again to coat the chicken, then add 2 cups of water. The chicken should be ready when the water has evaporated, if not add more water and continue to cook.

2
Put the rice in a pan, add 1 tsp of salt and cover with water (the level of water should be 1cm above the rice). Bring to the boil. After 10 minutes stir, add 4tbsp of oil and then leave covered (using a tea towel and lid) until the water has been fully absorbed.

3
Place an ice cube in a small bowl and add the saffron threads. When the ice has melted, the water will have taken on the colour and taste of the saffron. In a small pan heat 1 tbsp of oil and add the (washed) barberries and 1tsp of sugar. Cook for 1-2 minutes, remove from heat and pour in the saffron flavoured water.

Serve the chicken and rice on plates with the zereshk (barberries) on top.

meat

MNAZLIT AL-BATINJAN

HANA
SYRIA

SERVES
4

PREP.
20 MIN

COOK
25 MIN

I learned how to cook when I was 17. Most girls in Syria actually start when they are 10. My whole family is good at cooking. When I don't know what to cook, I call my siblings. This recipe is important because the food is from generations ago, yet, it remains unchanged. There are two main reasons why it is important: preservation of heritage and for the health of my children.

My life in Syria was perfect because before I was married, my parents did everything for me. When I married, my husband was controlling. He wouldn't let me work. Right before I left for Greece, there were a lot of problems in our family. I left with my children to find a better life.
I moved to Iraq for a little while before going to Turkey. In Iraq, I saw people die. We spent one month in Turkey, then took a boat to Chios and stayed there for four months. The cousin of my mother had a friend with family in Eleonas in Athens, so we came to stay with them. It was crowded at first, because we stayed in the container with other family members.

My life here is not very good. I'm alone with just my children. I have diabetes, high blood pressure, and disc problems in my back. Since coming here my sugar levels are sometimes over 400 mg/dL, so I must go to the hospital often. I imagine going back to Syria but I know that I cannot. I came to Europe for my children. We were rich in Syria, we did not come to Europe for money but for peace. I hope to be with my siblings in Germany. I want my children to do whatever they want to do, but first, they must study and I encourage them to also do what they enjoy, like theatre.

INGREDIENTS

2 eggplants/
aubergines, halved
2 tbsp vegetable oil
225g/8oz tomato
passata
125g/4oz mozzarella,
grated
1 onion, finely chopped
250g/8oz minced beef
4 tbsp parsley, freshly
chopped

STEPS

1 Preheat oven to 200°C/400 °F. Heat the oil in a large non-stick frying pan over a medium/high heat. Fry the eggplant halves on both sides until soft. Remove from heat. With a spoon press down the center of each half to create a space to fill with the minced meat mixture later.

2 In a separate pan, cook the onion, minced beef and parsley together until cooked.

3 Pour the tomato passata into a large baking dish. Place the eggplant halves into the dish and fill each eggplant half with the minced meat mixture. Generously sprinkle mozzarella on top.

4 Bake for approximately 10 minutes or until the cheese is melted.

Serve with your choice of rice, salad, and/or natural yogurt.

ACHAR GOSHT

TAHIRA
PAKISTAN

SERVES
6

PREP.
30 MIN

COOK
45 MIN

I am from Karachi, the city with the highest population in Pakistan. I have been in Eleonas since July 2017 with my husband and my 11 year-old son. I have another son of 13 years who lives in a refugee camp in Paris. We wish to be together in the near future.

In my country I was a cultured and educated woman. I studied economics and then studied for a master degree. I had a privileged position. My husband had a shop. In Pakistan I didn't cook, I didn't have the time. I learned to cook on the way, especially here in Greece. I had to do it to feed my family. Before I was working in a bank and now I sell food in the camp. It's a way to make some more money every month.

We had to flee because Pakistan is a very corrupt country where you cannot move forward. I love my country but we couldn't have a future there. My parents are Afghans, so I also speak Farsi besides Urdu.

In the future I want my family to be united and to have the freedom to travel around Europe.

INGREDIENTS

50g/1.75oz Achar Gosht Spice Mix*
1kg/2lb beef (or chicken/mutton if preferred) diced
200g/7oz natural yogurt
2 medium onions, sliced
1 tbsp paprika
1 tbsp turmeric
5-6 medium tomatoes, peeled and diced
6 cloves garlic, crushed
5g/0.18oz fresh ginger, peeled and finely chopped
8-10 small green chilli peppers, finely chopped
1-2 tbsp lemon juice
parsley
cooking oil
salt

*See index page. 96

STEPS

1 Ground the Achar Gosht Spice Mix spices together, using a pestle and mortar if available. Marinate the beef with the yogurt and half of the spices for about 30 minutes.

2 Heat a generous amount of oil in a pan and add the onions, paprika, tumeric and salt. While the onions and spices are frying, blend the tomatoes with 100ml/3fl oz of water. Add the garlic and ginger and blend again.

3 When the onion is ready (after about 15 minutes), add the remaining Spice Mix and the blended tomato mixture and cook for a further 5 minutes.

4 Stir in the beef, cover with a lid and cook for 20 minutes on a medium heat. Add the green chilli peppers and lemon juice and cook for 10 more minutes at a low tempeature, still covered. Finally, sprinkle with chopped parsley.

Serve with a side salad of thinly sliced fresh vegetables.

LAHMAJOUN

SARWAT
IRAQ

SERVES
4

PREP.
50 MIN

COOK
15 MIN

I learned how to cook in a pizza shop in Baghdad. I started by washing the dishes. Every day I went one hour early to learn how to cook just watching the chef do his job. I remember the silence in the shop at that time, only interrupted by the sound of the knives cutting the ingredients. I started making my own food and I eventually became head chef.

In Iraq the biggest problem is the militant groups. They tell you that they are the 'true Muslims' and misuse the words of Islam to get you to fight with them. I didn't want to kill or be killed so I left.

My life in Europe will be very good, everything is changing. Here I feel safe. I just got my residency. I want to study arts, I want to draw. For that I have to find a job, to pay my life, because art for me is love and you don't sell your love. The ability to paint I got from God, nobody told me how to do it and that's why I would never sell it. If someone likes my art, I give it as a present.

Where I would like to work? In a pizza shop, of course, because when I make pizza I am happy.

INGREDIENTS

400g/14oz (1 can)
tomato passata
1kg/2lb white flour
1kg minced meat
4tbsp vegetable oil
1tbsp olive oil
2 tsp salt
1 tbsp sugar
1 tbsp dried yeast
1 sprig fresh oregano
1 handful fresh basil,
finely chopped
2 tbsp thyme leaves
1 celery stalk
1 spring onion
2 medium sized
tomatoes

STEPS

1 On a clean work surface create a mound out of the flour and make a well in the middle. Into the well add 250ml of water, sugar, salt, vegetable oil, yeast and mix. Knead the mixture until a soft dough is formed. Cover with cling film until the dough is firm and bouncy, approximately 40 minutes.

2 To make the sauce combine the tomato passata, oregano, basil, thyme, salt, sugar and olive oil in a bowl. Then, for the meat topping, put the oil and salt into a frying pan and partially cook the minced meat over a medium heat.

3 Pre-heat oven to 240°/475°F. On a floured surface, roll out the dough to a thickness of ½cm to the sizes and shapes of your choice. Spread a layer of the sauce onto the bases and then cover with the minced meat.

4 Cook in the oven until golden brown, approximately 15 minutes.

To serve finely dice celery, onion and tomato and sprinkle on top.

KOTLET

LEILA
IRAN

SERVES
4

PREP.
25 MIN

COOK
25 MIN

I learned to cook a little from cooking with my mum. But it was really when I was a student, living away from my family that I learned more. I also learnt a lot from the mother of my husband. I met Ali when I was a student, six years ago. We met at a friends' house and for the next four years we remained friends in secret, because it is difficult to be with a man in Iran unless you are married. I would often ask his mum for help when I was cooking. He and his mother are very close and sometimes, if I had a problem with Ali and we weren't talking to each other, I would speak to his mum. We became good friends and would go out together. I would often ring her when I was cooking.

When we were in Iran we were engaged but we had to leave before we could marry. My father was very upset by that and did not talk to me for a long time. Earlier this year we went to visit mine and Ali's mum in Georgia for Ali's birthday. They didn't tell us, but they had arranged for us a marriage ceremony as a surprise!

Because there is no 'war' in Iran, it is not seen as a very dangerous country. Those of us here had more serious problems with the government. Iran is an Islamic country with special rules such as requiring women to wear the hijab, only allowing certain types of music, only permitting certain types of work, etc. In Iran you cannot say anything. You must accept the rules. They don't want the world to know the real situation. It's like America: on the TV everything looks perfect and beautiful but, in reality it's not like that. For that, I think America and Iran are not so dissimilar.

We are also not safe in Greece; we cannot say what we really think for fear that they will hurt our families who are still living in Iran.

INGREDIENTS

3 medium potatoes
1 red onion
200g/7oz minced beef
2 medium eggs
2 tbsp white flour
1 tbsp ground black pepper
1 tbsp turmeric
1 tbsp salt
sunflower oil
1 lemon
2 or 3 tomatoes (optional)

STEPS

1
Peel and wash the potatoes. Then finely grate on the smallest hole. Peel and grate the onion on the medium hole. Put the grated onion and potato into a large bowl, then add all the ingredients apart from the oil. Mix together well using your hands until everything is combined. Leave for 5-10 minutes to allow the flavours to marinade the meat.

2
Turn on the hob to a medium-high heat to warm up. Place the pan on the heat and add enough oil to cover the pan. Leave to heat up while the mixture is marinating. The oil should be very hot when you start frying.

3
Take the mixture and make small balls in your hands. Then flatten them out into patties in the palm of your hand. Place the patties (as many as you can fit easily) into the pan. They should sizzle immediately.

4
Fry the kotlets for about 5-7 minutes (turning occasionally) until golden-brown in colour on both sides. Remove from heat. To eat with the Kotlet, you can cut tomatoes into thick slices and fry in the same oil as the Kotlet.

Serve the patties with the fried tomato and slices of lemon, and eat with bread, rice or chips.

AUSHAK

ADELE
AFGHANISTAN

SERVES
6

PREP.
45 MIN

COOK
30 MIN

When I was a girl I used to watch my mother cooking and she taught me at the same time. At the beginning I learned to cook eggs, potatoes and so on. For me cooking is really important because it's a tool for life. I feel proud of making food that will be enjoyed by the people who visit my house.

In Afghanistan I had a normal life. The only problem was that my husband was a policeman. Because of that, they used to call my phone and make threats, saying that they would kill me and my family. The Taliban killed my father-in-law and shot my husband in the leg just because of his work and because he studied in Russia. For those reasons we decided to go to Iran and after 10 years there we had to move to Europe because life in Iran wasn't easy either.

From Iran, we went to the border of Turkey and we walked through the mountains for 10 hours while it was snowing. After that we took a bus to Istanbul and stayed there for 15 days, moved to Ismir and then we took a boat for 3 hours with other 100 people. We arrived to Chios, we stayed there less than a week and we moved to Athens. We lived (the 5 of us) in a tent for 3 months at the port and then we were moved to Eleonas.

My life in Athens is ok but here we cannot build a future when there are no jobs and there are a lot of Greek people sleeping on the streets. I only want a normal life and a normal job, we don't need much money. We are only interested in a healthy life and having the legal papers to be treated as normal and study and work like the rest of the citizens. On top of that, I would like to have a home where I can receive guests and cook them something tasty.

INGREDIENTS

2kg/4lb white flour
3kg/6lb leeks
1kg/2lb natural yogurt
1 clove garlic, crushed
3 large onions, finely
choppped
500g/1lb minced lamb
2 tsp turmeric
1 medium green chilli
pepper, finely chopped
4 medium tomatoes,
finely diced
2 tbsp tomato puree
170g/6oz peas
400ml/14fl oz
vegetable oil
salt
1/2 tsp pepper

STEPS

1
The dough: Put the flour in a bowl and stir in 1tsp of salt. Gradually pour in about 450ml/3/4pint water, kneading until the dough has a smooth, non-sticky consistency. Roll it out to a thickness of no more than 3mm/0.1inch. Cut the dough in circles, using a glass cup, and leave to rest.

2
Leek filling: Wash the leeks and finely chop. Pour 2 tbsp of oil into a pan and fry the leeks, adding 1 tsp of salt.
Yogurt: Combine the yogurt, garlic and 1/2 tsp salt in a bowl.
Minced Meat: Fry the onion until golden. Add the meat, turmeric, green chilli pepper, tomatoes, tomato puree and stir. Pour in 300ml/1/2pint of water and bring to the boil. Reduce the temperature and simmer for 10 minutes.
Peas: In a separate saucepan, boil some water and add the frozen peas. Cook for 5 minutes, then drain. Add the peas to the minced meat and mix.

3
Aushaks: Fill a large pan with water, add 2 tsp of salt and bring to the boil. Take 1 tablespoonful of leek filling and place on a circle of dough. Moisten the edges of the dough with water and fold the dough circle in half, pressing down at the edges. Repeat until all the dough and leak filling has been used. Once the water is boiling gently place the aushaks into the pot. Approximately 30 aushaks can be cooked at a time. After around 2 minutes the aushaks will start to rise and fall. Wait 2 more minutes and then remove.

Serve on a large platter. First create a base with yogurt. Then place the aushaks on top and cover them with the meat and peas sauce.

seafood

MFUMBWA & FISH

**LYDIE
DEM. REP. OF THE
CONGO**

**SERVES
6**

**PREP.
10 MIN**

**COOK
25 MIN**

When I was 15 years old my mother started teaching me how to cook. Every year we have a carnival in Congo and she taught me how to cook for this party. For us cooking is a way to gather the family, especially, for big celebrations.

In Congo I had a husband but after my life became really difficult. My husband disappeared and things got worse.

One night I was sleeping in my home and some people came and knocked on the door. They asked where my husband was. As he wasn't there they started asking for money. I didn't want to give them any and they started punching me. They took out a knife and cut my face under my left eye. A friend took me to the hospital. I had to leave the country. The same friend helped me get out of the country and to Turkey.

In Greece things are okay. We need to establish here and see what the future has for me and my baby Benjamin.

INGREDIENTS

**250g/8oz mfumbwa
-edible vegetable
leaves, found wild in
forests throughout
tropical Africa.
(spinach can be used as
a substitute)
300g/10oz crunchy
peanut butter
300g/10oz white fish
1 white onion
3-5 spring onions
2 small green chilli
peppers
2 tbsp tomato puree
175ml/6fl oz palm oil
1/2 stock cube
1 tsp nutmeg
2 garlic cloves
1 tsp salt**

STEPS

1 Wash the fumbua in hot water and drain.

2 Cut the white fish into small pieces and add finely chopped onion, green peppers, spring onions and garlic.

3 To this mix add the fumbua, tomato puree, peanut butter, palm oil, stock cube and salt. Add 750ml/1 1/2 pints of water.

4 Cook the mixture on high heat and stir non-stop for 25 minutes, or until most of the water has evaporated.

Serve with bread.

SHRIMP BIRYANI

ARIF
PAKISTAN

SERVES
4

PREP.
15 MIN

COOK
30 MIN

I am from a frontier tribe from Karachi City. Previously I lived in UK for four years. I was cooking in an Indian restaurant. When I cook I love to bring the Pakistani and Indian style of food together.

I was deported from the UK back to Pakistan. I couldn't live in Pakistan. Life there is very difficult. You can have a good life only if you have money or power. My life started to be even harder after I got married. I had serious issues with my wife's family. I decided to move with my wife and 4 kids to Europe.

Life in Greece is good but since my wife is in Switzerland it has been a bit complicated because I have to raise my kids by myself and I wasn't ready for that.

I will do everything to make sure that my children have opportunities and a proper education. My children are my future.

INGREDIENTS

30g/1oz ginger, grated
1 garlic clove, crushed
1 green chili, finely diced
175g/6oz natural yogurt
2 medium potatoes, diced
1 medium onion, finely chopped
2 tomatoes, diced
25-30 peeled shrimps
1 tbsp Garam Masala*
250g/8oz basmati rice
olive oil
salt
fresh coriander

*See index page. 96

STEPS

1
To make the sauce, mix the ginger, garlic, chili pepper, 1 tbsp oil and salt together. Fold into the yoghurt until combined. Refridgerate.

2
In a saucepan, bring some water to the boil and add the potatoes. Cook until soft, then drain.

3
In a pan over a high heat, brown the onion in 2 tbsp oil until soft. Add the tomatoes, shrimps and Garam Masala and fry for a further 10 minutes until the shrimp are cooked.

4
Next, add the cooked potatoes and gently stir in the yogurt sauce. Reduce the heat. Meanwhile, boil the rice and season with salt. Finally, stir the rice into the shrimp/potato mixture.

Serve with the chopped fresh coriander.

veggie

UGALI & SAUCE

VINCENT
UGANDA

SERVES
4

PREP.
10 MIN

COOK
25 MIN

My mother taught me how to cook. In my family I have two sisters and two brothers. My sister got married so I had to help her cook when I was 16 years old. I love cooking because I do it with so much love that after it is a big pleasure to eat it. People don't put much effort in cooking but I do and I can feel it in the taste.

My life in Uganda was really good but I had an important problem there and I had to leave. I wanted to stay but I couldn't at the same time. To escape I went to Sudan and then to Turkey and from Turkey I went by boat to Samos, Greece. There were 12 people in the boat and we didn't know how to operate it. Luckily, God helped us to find the way. I am a strong believer that at the end everything will be ok. Life in Greece is ok. Everywhere there are good people and bad people but here it is ok. I do weight lifting and enjoy doing that, as well as going to school for Greek lessons and classical music. I studied music for four years.

I will stay here in Greece because I have no choice and because it is God's plan. In the future I would love to speak Greek fluently so I can focus on getting an accounting degree. I would also like to find a woman and have one more child. I have a daughter back in Uganda who stayed with her mother. I am really proud of her; she is 16 and number one in her class.

INGREDIENTS

For the sauce:
200g/7oz red kidney beans
1/2 onion, chopped
1 medium tomato, diced
1 vegetable stock cube
1 tbsp cooking oil
1 tsp salt

For the ugali :
500g/1lb cornmeal
600ml/1pint water

STEPS

1 The sauce: To a pot, add the red kidney beans and cover with water. Bring to the boil and simmer until the beans are soft in the middle. Drain, reserving around one glass of the now flavoured water.

2 Fry the onion over high heat until soft, then add the tomato. Once softened, crush the tomatoes to form a sauce-like consistency. Add the cooked beans, stock cube, salt and bean-flavoured water. Stir and cook at a high temperature for 5 to 10 minutes.

3 The Ugali: Bring the water to the boil and then slowly add the cornmeal. Stir the mixture constantly for approximately 10 minutes. The consistency should be firm but fluffy. Add either extra water or cornmeal as necessary.

4 Serve the Ugali on a plate with the bean sauce on top.

62

Ugali can be eaten cold (mixed with yogurt) or warm (with the bean sauce).

BANJAN BORANI

MOHAMMAD
AFGHANISTAN

SERVES
4

PREP.
30 MIN

COOK
45 MIN

I taught myself how to cook. I started when my father died and my mother married another man. I was young but taught myself how to cook for myself. I had to try a lot before I learnt. Cooking has two meanings for me - responsibility and relaxation. In Afghanistan I had the best life. I was doing a bit of everything, I didn't have a specific job, I was a handyman. I left Afghanistan and went to Iran, and then to Turkey. I went to Lesvos by boat then to Athens. It took a total of 2 months from Iran to Athens. I lived in Iran for 6-7 years before leaving.

Thanks be to God that I have a relaxed and normal life in Greece with no problems. I feel safe here.

I want to study and have an education to find my way and to solve my problems. I want all my sons to be like the volunteers and turn around and help people as they are. I'm not looking to earn money, I just want my sons to become good people and help the people in need. I hope they are not like me who couldn't study; I want them to be good humans. I want them to have open minds and to be brave.

INGREDIENTS

**2kg/4lb eggplant/
aubergine, sliced
1kg/2lb tomatoes, diced
1 green bell pepper,
chopped
2 brown onions, finely
chopped
1 tsp salt
1 tbsp cumin
1 tbsp black pepper
sunflower oil
natural yogurt to serve**

STEPS

1 Cut the eggplants into 2cm/1/2 inch slices. Sprinkle liberally with salt and leave them to ooze the water for half an hour and then pat them dry.

2 While waiting for the eggplants, mix the chopped tomatoes and green pepper together in a bowl. Add the salt, cumin and black pepper. In a pan fry the onions in 1 tbsp oil until golden brown, then add the tomato and pepper mixture.

3 In separate pan, fry the sliced eggplant in oil on both sides until browned and remove, after around 10 minutes. In a baking tray layer the eggplants and then the tomato mixture on top.

4 Bake at 180°C/350°F for 20 minutes.

Serve on a bed of yogurt.

LAHORI CHIKAR CHOLAY

SHAMAN
PAKISTAN

SERVES
6

PREP.
3 HRS

COOK
2 HRS

My husband taught me how to cook. Cooking is important for health and it bonds the family and keeps us healthy. We become united through cooking and eating.

My life in Pakistan was good. The only problem was the fighting between the Shia and Sunnis of Islam. My husband was attacked. When we left Pakistan we went to Iran by plane. We then had to drive for 13 hours and walk for 15 hours through the mountains to Turkey. We stayed in a house there for five nights. In the night we took a boat across the Mediterranean Sea to Kos, an island in Greece. From Kos we took a ferry to Athens.

My life in Athens is good. There are no conflicts here between the Shias and Sunnis. Although my life is good, I do not have any papers yet so I am not allowed to have a job. I cannot move countries and will possibly have to stay in Athens.

My children are here with me. They are studying in school and will learn many languages like Greek and English. They will have jobs and will be married with kids one day.

INGREDIENTS

500g/1lb chickpeas
1 tsp baking powder
2 medium onions
1 tbsp cumin seeds
2 tbsp fresh ginger
2 cloves garlic, crushed
4 green chili peppers
1 tbsp turmeric powder
1 1/2 tbsp Chinese salt
1 1/2 tbsp black pepper
1 tsp cloves
1 tsp coriander seeds
1/2 tbsp cinnamon
1/2 tbsp fennel powder
250ml/8fl oz sunflower oil
fresh coriander and pita bread to serve.

STEPS

1 Preparation: Simmer chickpeas with the baking powder for 2 to 3 hours.

2 Crush the cumin and coriander seed with the cloves using a pestle and mortar. Separately, blend the onion, garlic, ginger and green chili peppers. Add the crushed spices and turmeric and mix well.

3 To this mixture, add the Chinese salt, black pepper, cinnamon and fennel powder along with the sunflower oil.

4 When the chickpeas are almost cooked stir in the spice mixture and cook for an additional 15 minutes on a medium heat. Add salt according to desired taste.

Serve in bowls with coriander and pita.

JEZ-MEZ

ALYA
SYRIA

SERVES
4

PREP.
10 MIN

COOK
20 MIN

I got married when I was 15 years old. I had to learn to cook with my mum and my mother-in-law. The first time I tried to cook I made beans and they burned, but with time I learned. Like in any Arabic country, in Syria we live to eat.

In Syria I was a hairdresser and a makeup artist. There I had everything, but because of the bombs, the war and the deaths I moved. I left because of my kids; I didn't want anything to happen to them. We moved from Turkey to Chios, and from Chios to Athens in September 2017.

In Chios our life was very bad. In Eleonas, at the beginning, I was participating in every activity but now I spend more time by myself. I go to my English classes and I take care of my kids. My husband disappeared 5 years ago and I never again heard from him, or if he died or not. I am not waiting for him. If he is gone there is a reason.

I don't know in which country I will end up in but my dream is to have a hairdressing shop. Will I marry again? I don't know. If somebody special to love appears, I would marry again.

INGREDIENTS

2 red onions
5-6 tomatoes
7 medium eggs
salt
sunflower oil

STEPS

1 Finely chop the onions and tomatoes. Cook in a saucepan on a high heat until soft and juicy. Add a little salt and then take off the heat.

2 Whisk the eggs together with some salt. Place a frying pan on a high heat and add enough oil to fill the pan. Leave until the oil is very hot. Then add the eggs and scramble them - stirring quickly with a wooden spoon. Once scrambled, take off the heat.

3 Put the tomatoes back on a medium heat and stir in the eggs. Once hot, take off the heat.

4 For more flavour, you can sprinkle spices on top such as garam masala, allspice or paprika, and stir in before serving

Serve with bread.

MSA'A

HOUDA
SYRIA

SERVES
6

PREP.
15 MIN

COOK
20 MIN

I learned to cook with my mother and with my grandmother. I have huge luck in having my mother here in Greece with me. Besides her I am with my husband and my two kids.

For me cooking is really important. I learned by heritage, it's a knowledge that is transmitted from woman to woman. In Afrin (Kurdistan), we keep making recipes from the past, from our grandparents and even more. You can say that it is history, like in a museum. When I cook I feel free. I put all my energy on that, I focus completely and it is a lot of fun.

I made the same trip to Greece as my container mates. After leaving Syria we met on the boat that was taking us from Turkey to Lesbos. Since then we have been together in the islands and in Athens. With them and other families coming from Afrin we have made a new family. We came to Eleonas in October 2017.

I don't want to be in Greece, I want to be in Germany as soon as possible to have a quiet future with better conditions for everyone.

INGREDIENTS

1kg/2lb eggplants/ aubergines
1,5kg/3lb tomatoes
1 large onion, sliced
1 clove garlic, sliced
1 tbsp paprika
1 tbsp coriander seeds, ground
sunflower oil
olive oil
salt
1 tsp pepper
1 lemon
parsley

STEPS

1 Peel and wash the eggplants. Cut in half and then slice. Fry in a good amount of sunflower oil.

2 In a big pan, add half a cup of olive oil over medium heat. When the oil is hot add the onion. When the onion it's almost cooked, add the garlic and some salt.

3 After approximately 5 more minutes, when the garlic and onion are golden in colour, add the tomatoes, paprika and pepper.

4 Once the juice/water of the tomato has evaporated, add the eggplant, season with salt and leave on high heat for 5-7 minutes.

70

Serve with lemon and chopped parsley.

BOLANI KACHALOO & GANDANA

AMIR
AFGHANISTAN

SERVES
8

PREP.
30 MIN

COOK
10 MIN

I learned to cook while in the camp because my wife had done all the cooking before and now she is in Germany with my young son. The first time I cooked, the food wasn't very good but the second time around I thought it was perfect. My favourite thing to cook and eat is rice. I think that cooking is important because it means providing for your family and your city. Cooking is significant for the culture of Afghanistan. It means forgiveness and peace during times of trouble. It is also a tool of unity for families.

I am from the city of Mazar in Afghanistan. I love the culture of Mazar because of its long history. One thing we are known for is our care for sheep. Both big and small; we watch, care and sell sheep which is what I did as well. At home I lived with my mother and my father. I spent a lot of time with them and I miss them now. I want to see my parents and my city again one day.

From Turkey to Lesvos I took a boat for 2-3 hours and it was very dangerous. There were 80-90 people squished onto one small boat. Life in Greece is not bad but I don't want to be here. I don't like that my family isn't here. In Afghanistan for work I did a little bit of everything. I am willing to do anything. I especially want to be a gardener where I can plant trees and plants. But most of all, I would like to own a car wash like I did back in Afghanistan.

INGREDIENTS

425g/14oz white flour
1 tsp salt
1 tsp olive oil

500g/1lb potatoes
1/2 cup fresh cilantro/coriander, finely chopped
4 spring onions, finely chopped
75ml/5 tbsp olive oil
1 1/2 tsp salt
1 tsp black pepper

STEPS

1 In a large bowl, mix together the flour and salt. Slowly add 250ml/8fl oz of water and a teaspoon of oil until the dough is smooth and elastic. Knead the dough for 10-15 minutes. Then set aside in a bowl and cover with a cloth for 1hr.

2 Boil the potatoes until soft. Remove from the water and take off the skins. Place the cooked potatoes into bowl and mix in the cilantro/coriander, spring onions, oil, salt, and black pepper. Crush the potatoes and mix using your hands.

3 Take a small ball of dough and roll out flat (sized to fit the frying pan). Evenly spread about 4 tbsp of potato mixture onto the dough. Then fold the dough in half, pressing down the edges.

4 Pour oil into a frying pan on a medium heat. Place the Bolani into the pan and fry until lightly browned on both sides, flipping periodically. Repeat until mixture is finished.

ASH-E RESHTEH

SARA
AFGHANISTAN

SERVES
6

PREP.
10 HRS

COOK
2 HRS

The dish is called Ash-e. I don't think it belongs to a specific country but it became an Afghani or Iranian dish. I learned cooking by not having anybody to cook for me. Cooking or food in general means a lot to my culture and we really value food. I think we have one of the best cuisines in the world. My life was very complicated in Afghanistan because I wasn't safe there. It felt home and nowhere else can be like Afghanistan for me. You always have to miss something, for example here in Greece I am safe but it doesn't feel like home.

We started our journey by going to Iran then Turkey. We went by boat to Greece to the Island of Lesvos and finally from Lesvos to Athens. My life is fine in Greece but since I have been here for a long time, I am really tired of the system in this country. Everything takes forever and this is what makes my life harder.

In the future I do not know what to look forward to because as a refugee my life is very unclear. Yet, because I am a refugee and I can fully understand how it feels to be one, I want to work for refugees or immigrants one day *(Sara is now in Germany with her family!)*.

INGREDIENTS

60g/2oz dried chickpeas
60g/2oz dried red kidney beans
250g/8oz spaghetti/ linguine
2 large onions, finely chopped
6 gloves garlic, finely chopped
1 tbsp dried mint
3 tbsp olive oil
salt
pepper
yogurt (to serve)

STEPS

1 Place the chickpeas and kidney beans in a large container and cover well with water. Leave overnight (at least 8 hours) to soak. Drain, discarding the water.

2 Put the chickpeas and beans into a large pot, cover with several inches of water, and bring to a boil. Reduce the heat and simmer until they reach your desired tenderness- between 1 1/2 to 2 hours.

3 Break the spaghetti into thirds. In slightly salted water, boil the spaghetti until tender and drain.

4 While the spaghetti is cooking, heat the olive oil in a pot and stir in the onions. Cook and stir until onion has turned translucent, about 5 minutes. Add the garlic and cook for a further minute. Stir in the chickpeas, kidney beans and spaghetti. Add salt, pepper and dried mint.

Serve with yogurt.

veggie

LENTIL SOUP

HASSAN
SYRIA

SERVES
4

PREP.
15 MIN

COOK
30 MIN

I was born in Syria. I learned how to cook from my mom, fiancée, YouTube and from my mistakes. I lived alone for 8 years, so I had to cook for myself. Cooking is an art. An art I enjoy. Damascus, the city I come from, is famous for ice bakdash (ice cream). In Syria cooking brings family together. Sometimes as many as 50 family members and friends meet up to eat.

I left Syria with the help of smugglers. I had to cross through 9 countries by land to get to Greece. It has already been 8 years since I left Syria. It wasn't a life choice to move to Europe. I had to do it, I had no options. I would rather be in a peaceful Syria than in Europe. Here I don't have my family and that makes all the difference. If they would be here with me I would be happy. The final decision is up to God. I believe in him.

Eventually I would like to go back to Turkey. I lived there for two years and I learned how to speak Turkish. I enjoyed my time there. I am a mechanic and would like to open a mechanic shop in the future.

INGREDIENTS

2 onions, finely chopped
300g/10oz small
red/brown lentils
(pre-soaked)
175g/6oz short grain rice
1 chicken stock cube
(substitute with
vegetable stock for a
vegetarian option)
3 tbsp oil
salt and pepper
1 lemon
pita bread

Optional:
1/2 tsp cumin
1/2 tsp turmeric

STEPS

1 Heat the oil in a pot and add the finely chopped onions.

2 Once the onions become translucent, add the stock cube, rice and lentils. Pour in 1l/32fl oz water and bring to boil.

3 Make sure to keep stirring so that the rice and lentils don't stick to the bottom of the pan.

4 When the rice and lentils have almost cooked, add salt and pepper (and optional spices) to taste.

Serve in bowls with lemon wedges and pita on the side.

sweets and drinks

SOLEH ZARD

RANA
AFGHANISTAN

SERVES
6

PREP.
10 MIN

COOK
40 MIN

I was born in Afghanistan. I learned to cook with my mother when I was 12. I used to watch her cooking and learned from that. I never asked her how to do it, I just watched her cook. The first food that I made was potato stew and I made it as a surprise. It was for seven people and they really loved it. The food I am cooking is very important for us; we make it for important occasions like Ramadan and Muharram.

My life in Afghanistan was very good but we had to escape because of the war, because of the Taliban. I lost 3 brothers because of the war. One was a doctor and when he was on a plane on the way to help some people, the plane was shot. My other brother was sick and the Taliban had blocked medicine and doctors from coming into our town so he died at only 9 years old. The youngest one was 2.5 years old and he was shot.

We left for Iran with my father, his two wives and the rest of my siblings (6 brothers and 1 sister). There I lived for 24 years, got married and had 4 children. We had to leave because my husband didn't have papers and if the government caught him he would have been deported back to Afghanistan. My husband is already in Austria and we are asking for family reunification to live all together there.

My life in Greece is normal. I do the housekeeping, cook and I take care of my kids. At the camp I participate on the Project Elea activities, especially the women's group. I like it, it's time for me. My dream is to be with my family again.

INGREDIENTS

200g/7oz rice
1 tsp saffron thread
270g/9.5oz sugar
1 tsp cardamom powder
pinch of cinnamon

STEPS

1 Put the rice in a bowl and cover with water. Leave it for 5 hours to allow the rice to soften.

2 Mix the saffron threads with a teaspoon of sugar and, using the back of a spoon, mash them together. Afterwards, place in a little cup and add 80ml/3fl oz of wáter and cover it.

3 Bring a pan of water to the boil. Drain the rice, add to the pan and stir constantly at a medium heat. One way to recognize if you need to continue to stir is if the rice sinks. After 10 minutes, add 200g/7oz sugar. Simmer for 15 more minutes, stirring occasionally, then add the cardamom powder.

4 Keep stirring until most of the water has evaporated, then add 70g/2.5 oz of sugar. The rice should be very soft and the grains easy to crush. If necessary, add more water and continue to cook for longer.

5 20 minutes later, when the rice is ready, add the liquid saffron and continue stirring for 5 more minutes. Keep a small amount of liquid on top of rice to keep moisture. Garnish with cinnamon and serve.

80

TURTA

NAZANIN
IRAQ (KURDISH)

SERVES
8

PREP.
30 MIN

COOK
0 MIN

I love sweet things; to cook them and eat them. I have been learning through the years with my sister, friends and school. Now that I am older, I like watching cooking TV shows and later I try them with friends and family. For me cooking is to show love, it's sharing. In Iraq, we cook sweet things for those we love a lot. In Iraq my life was good, very good, until everything bad began.

I was a Biology teacher and I lost my job. Everything is war. Everyone is fighting. To come to Athens first we went on a small boat to Samos where the situation was horrible. We slept in tents that were completely wet. After that we moved to Athens in a big boat. Our life is not good here. We live in a container that is impossible to keep clean, it's very humid and that's why we have mosquitos all the time. In the camp the only good things are the volunteers. In Athens the main problem is that there are no jobs and not all the Greek people want us here.

In the future I want to move to Germany with my husband and 2 kids. My daughter has a problem in one of her eyes that could make her blind if she doesn't have surgery. We have been waiting for a doctor to treat her for almost 2 years in Athens. We know that in Germany health is a priority and that's why we would love to move there. My husband used to live in Germany, he speaks German very well and he will have a good chance to get a job there.

INGREDIENTS

600ml/1pint milk
3 tbsp flour
2 tbsp sugar
500g/1lb of rectangular tea biscuits
500g almonds
2 tbsp cacao powder
2 bananas, ripe
250g/8oz cream

STEPS

1 Mix the milk, flour and sugar in a bowl until creamy.

2 Place a layer of the tea biscuits in a baking tray to form the base of the cake. Pour the milk mixture on top of the biscuit base.

3 Add a layer of almonds (whole or grated) and a sliced banana. To the cream mix in the cacao powder and spoon a layer on top of the almonds and banana.

4 For the final layer, add the remaining almonds and bananas. Chill and then it is ready to eat.

BAKA

MALIK
IVORY COAST

SERVES
4

PREP.
5 MIN

COOK
10 MIN

I didn't like to cook. In my country my wife cooked for me but when I arrived in Greece I had to learn and cook for myself. Now I can cook different foods from Africa. There we used to gather all around food and celebrate.

In Ivory Coast I was married, I had a car, money. I used to work for the UN but I had my reasons to leave that I prefer not to tell. I had to lose everything to come here. For that, I went to Turkey for 5 months and after came to Greece.

My life in Greece is difficult but I am good thanks to God.

My dream is to bring my family here, they are the most important for me. Also to get a good job to have a better life.

INGREDIENTS

400g/13oz millet
1 can of condensed
milk (400g/13oz)
1 tsp salt
3 tsp sugar

STEPS

1 Put the millet and salt in a pan and cover with water. Bring to the boil, and stir as it boils for 8 minutes.

2 Add the sugar and reduce to a medium heat stirring constantly.

3 When the millet is completely soft (approximately another 2 minutes), reduce the heat further and add the milk.

4 Stir well, taste and add extra sugar if desired.

GOSH-E-FEEL

FARAHNAZ
AFGHANISTAN

SERVES
12

PREP.
2.5 HRS

COOK
20 MIN

I learned how to cook with my mother, in the same way that my mother learned from my grandmother. Now my young daughters (12, 11 and 7 years old) don't want to know anything about cooking. Only the oldest one, who is in Germany, wanted to follow the traditions and learned with me. When I cook I feel free. My husband was very popular so we used to eat with guests every day. Sometimes I cooked for more than 60 people by myself. In Afghanistan cooking is a way of socializing. That is why everyone is more overweight than in Europe!

In my country I was a kindergarten teacher at a school. I was working every day except Friday. Our trip here started by going from Afghanistan to Turkey and then through Greece to Macedonia by truck. We were stopped by police in Macedonia and deported back to Thessaloniki, Greece, where we spent 4 days in jail. From there they took us to Eleonas, where we have lived since October 2017.

I like Greece even though I have had bad experiences with some local people who don't want us here. Every day, I wake up very early to help my daughters prepare for school and after that I go to the camp football pitch to play badminton or volleyball with my friends. We have a teacher that says I am very good, even better than her. In the afternoons I go to the women's group and I study English until it's time to prepare dinner.

In the future, I would like to find a job to get a better life for my daughters. If it's in Greece it would be nice because they like living here, but it would be better if it is out of the camp. I don't know what is waiting for me but, if I could choose, I would like to work as a cook or kids teacher, like at home.

INGREDIENTS

500g/1lb flour
1/2 tsp ground cardamom
125ml/4fl oz oil
250ml/8fl oz milk
5 medium eggs

Icing sugar to decorate

Optional: Pistachios or walnuts, finely chopped

STEPS

1 Mix the flour and cardamom together. To a well in the flour, add the oil and mix. Next, add the milk and stir to make dough that can be kneaded.

2 Knead the dough until it has a smooth, firm texture (around 10 minutes). If the dough is too sticky, add more flour. Cover and allow to rest for 2 hours.

3 Divide the dough into smaller balls and use a rolling pin to flatten into pancakes around 1mm in thickness.

4 Cut the dough pieces into rounded rectangular shapes. Pinch along one edge so that it resembles the shape of an elephant ear. In Farsi Gosh-e-feel translates as 'ear of an elephant'.

5 Heat the oil in a pan. Fry the shaped dough for 2-3 minutes, rotating occasionally until golden. Remove excess oil and sprinkle with icing sugar to decorate.

Serve with finely chopped pistachios or walnuts.

SHIRPERA

**SHUKRIA
AFGHANISTAN**

**SERVES
6**

**PREP.
1.5 HRS**

**COOK
20 MIN**

My mother taught me how to cook Shirpera. It is a traditional dessert from Afghanistan. There are many different ways to make it, but this is my favourite.

I am happy when I cook. I love to cook for my family and friends. It makes me feel good.

Our situation in Afghanistan was really bad. I prefer not to think or talk about it. We came to Athens by boat. Here everything is better.

We don't know what is going to happen, we don't know anything about our future but we know what we want, we want to have a future where we can work, where we learn languages and where we can be accepted.

We have hope that everything is going to be ok.

INGREDIENTS

**250g/8oz milk powder
60g/2oz walnuts, crushed
60g/2oz almonds, crushed
1 tsp cardamom, ground
3-5 drops vanilla extract
250ml/8fl oz water
200g/7oz sugar
2 tbsp pistachios, crushed**

STEPS

1 In a bowl, mix the walnuts, almonds, cardamom and milk powder.

2 Put a pan onto medium heat and add the water and sugar. Stir continuously until the sugar has dissolved. Then let the mixture boil for 15 minutes, stirring occasionally. Turn off the heat and add the vanilla extract.

3 To the pot, add the dry milk powder and nut mixture. Mix everything together until a fudge forms. Coat a dish with a small amount of oil and pour the shirpera into the dish, flattening with a spoon.

4 Sprinkle with the pistachios to garnish, and set aside to cool for about 20 minutes. Finally refrigerate for at least one hour. Cut into pieces and serve.

VANILLA & CHOCOLATE SPONGE

DONYA
AFGHANISTAN

SERVES
12

PREP.
15 MIN

COOK
30 MIN

I learned how to cook from my mum. For me cooking is making something nice for my family and friends. It's not only about food, it's about love. I miss my life in Iran but I left because as someone from Afghanistan you do not have rights because they don't want us there. I wanted to donate blood and they didn't even want our blood. I left for the future of my children. What I miss the most is having my family all together. I miss having my mama to talk with. She understood that I had to make my children the priority. We didn't have the chance to study and I want different for my children.

It was a hard journey to Greece. We walked 18 hours from Iran to Turkey through the mountains. From there we went in a really small boat from Turkey to Greece. Luckily it was a calm night but the boat was packed with 92 people on it. Nothing bad happened but it was a tense situation. It took us 45 minutes to get to Chios. We stayed on the island 3 or 4 days before arriving in Athens. The only good thing of living here is the sun, I like that.

My family is now in Austria. I want my son to go to school and after to university. That's my dream.

INGREDIENTS

3 medium eggs
250ml/8fl oz milk
125ml/4fl oz oil
425g/14oz sugar
375g/12oz flour
1 tbsp vanilla powder
1 tbsp baking powder
7g/1/4oz cocoa powder

STEPS

1 Pre-heat the oven to 110°C/225°F. Take the eggs and separate the whites and yolks. Gentle whisk the egg whites together, then add the yolks, one by one. Continue whisking for 4-5minutes. Then, stir in the milk, oil and sugar.

2 In a separate bowl, combine the flour, vanilla powder and baking powder. Little by little, mix it into the egg/milk. Continue to mix for 5-6 minutes until smooth but not runny.

3 Divide the mixture into two. Grease a baking tray and pour in one half of the mixture. Add the cocoa powde to the remaining mixture, stir thoroughly and pour on top.

4 Place in the oven and bake for approximately 30 minutes.

ERK-SOUS

MOHAMMAD
SYRIA

SERVES
10

PREP.
10 MIN

COOK
24 HRS

Many people made Erk-Sous around me and I learned how to make it from them. In Syria we have a code and it says that there are two types of people: the ones who eat to live and the ones live to eat. For me, cooking is something like the spirit of teamwork because my wife and daughters always share in cooking with me. We help each other.

I am an electrical engineer, but I was simply teaching math and English before I came here. Before the war, I enjoyed my life with my family and friends. After the war, I just fought to survive. I was without my family for four years and then decided to come to Greece. From Syria I went to Turkey and then took a boat to Lesvos and another to Athens. My family is still in Syria and it is very difficult living away from them.

Here it is a refugee life: we live in containers instead of houses, we have roommates instead of family, we have to look for organizations and lawyers instead of ministry employees to help us with our issues and we have to spend our days looking for something.

Life in Greece is not ideal. It is hard for Greek people to find work, imagine for us. But when you are with your family, it doesn't matter the place. I just want to be with my family. I hope to go to a different European country, anywhere, as long as my family comes with me.

INGREDIENTS

200g of licorice root
Baking soda (1 teaspoon)
Rose petals (of 2 roses)
Sugar (if desired)

STEPS

1 Crush the licorice root.

2 Boil 10 cups of water and mix in the baking soda.

3 Turn off the heat, combine the licorice root with the water, and let it steep for 24 hours.

4 Take the petals of 2 roses and place in 6 cups of hot water (let it boil, then turn off burner and put on a lid). Let it sit for 10 minutes. Ad the rose water to the previous mixture.

Serve cold (with sugar as needed).

MINT TEA

SALAH
MOROCCO

SERVES
4

PREP.
5 MIN

COOK
1 HR

I am from Essaouira a small city in Morocco and am Sahawari by culture and tradition. We are famous for our tea. Every day we gather at least once to drink tea and to talk. Slowly this culture is changing though because people don't have the time anymore.

I studied law at university for 3 years and also belonged to many associations. With one political group, we created a petition demanding better access to education and healthcare for everyone. We had over 1 million signatures but it didn't even receive an answer. One by one all 23 people from our office were arrested.

With another organisiation we had organised an event to give free food during Ramadan but the mayor blocked it. One day after the police came to my house. They said that they had seen my post on Facebook complaining about the mayor, that the king had given the mayor his job and that we had to respect him. They took me to an office to be interrogated. A contact told me I was going to go to jail for a long time and asked if I had enough money to fix it. That is when I left.

Freedom and education is necessary to life wherever you are. People are being pushed to move. Everyone that is here in Greece was pushed; they didn't volunteer or choose. Eventually it doesn't matter if you don't like politics or are not interested in it; politics loves you, she lives with you and she controls you. I love Greece but the policies towards accepting refugees makes it difficult. I thought Europe respected human rights but it is all propaganda. It is run by some of the worst criminals in the world. They sell weapons to the Middle East. They make war with one hand and then help with the other.

INGREDIENTS

8 tbsp Chinese gunpowder green tea (compressed, dried tea leaves)
fresh spearmint leaves
1 stovetop-safe teapot

Optional:
Moroccan teapot (berrad)
tea glasses and serving tray

STEPS

1 Pour one glass of water into the teapot and add the green tea. Put the pot onto the fire or stove on a low heat. Once the pot begins to feel hot pour out the liquid. This cleans the tea leaves. Fill the pot with water and put back onto the heat. Traditionally the tea is slowly brewed for over an hour which adds to the depth of flavour.

2 Once the tea is hot, but not boiling, add the bunch of fresh mint leaves (prewashed). At this point you can also add sugar to taste. Slowly bring the tea to the boil. Once the tea has boiled for a few minutes it is ready to serve.

3 A Moroccan teapot has a built-in strainer which prevents tea leaves from pouring out of the pot. If your pot doesn't have this feature use a strainer intead.

4 If using a Moroccan teapot the long, curved spout will allow for accurate pouring from high above the glass. Tradionally the tea should be poured from at least an arms length above each glass. This aerates the tea and creates a nice foamy head.

Serve with dried fruits, nuts and/or sweets.

SPICE MIXES

MASALEDAR SINDHI BIRYANI MASALA
Chicken Biryani. Page 28

Mix together:

1 tsp red chili powder
1 tsp salt
2 tbsp fresh coriander, chopped
½ tsp turmeric powder
½ tsp ground cinnamon
4-6 pcs dried Plum
(pre-soaked)
2 green cardamom pods
2 black cardamom pods
4 cloves, ground
2 tsp cumin seeds
1 tsp garam masala
black pepper

ACHAR GOSHT
Achar Gosht. Page 46

Grind all ingredients together using a pestle and mortar:

2tbsp coriander seeds
2tsp jeera (cumin seeds)
1tsp shahi jeera (black cumin seeds)
1tsp black pepper
1 star anise
2tbsp garlic, crushed
1tsp mustard seeds
2 bay leaves
2½cm/1inch cinnamon stick
2 green cardamom pods

BIHARAT
Chicken Kabsa. Page 34

Dry roast the following in a pan over medium heat until slightly browned and aromatic:

2 tbsp black peppercorns
2 tbsp cumin seeds
1 tbsp coriander seeds
1 tbsp cloves
½ tsp cardamom pods
add:
1 tsp ground nutmeg
1 tsp ground cinnamon
2 tbsp paprika

and grind all ingredients together using a pestle and mortar.

GARAM MASALA
Shrimp Biryani. Page 58

Dry roast the following in a pan over medium heat until slightly browned and aromatic:

2 tsp cumin seeds
1 tsp coriander seeds
1 tsp cardamom pods
1 tsp black peppercorns
1/4 tsp cloves
add:
1/2 tsp ground cinnamon
1/4 tsp dried nutmeg
1/4 tsp turmeric

and grind all ingredients together using a pestle and mortar.

INDEX OF RECIPES

About us

Project Elea is a group of volunteers from around the world who have come together to work collaboratively with the residents of Eleonas Camp in Athens to improve living standards and community well being.

Working independently within the camp, Project Elea provides basic services such as clothing distribution, creative engagement through a varied schedule of skill sharing, culture and sports, as well as long-term development through education and employability programs.

Thank you

To Maria Ángeles Torres for your photography, creativity, hours of cooking and words of advice along the way. Thank you for trusting in this project from the very beginning. Your professionalism raised the bar and made us believe that it was real and possible.

To Susan Jane Gilman for kicking off the project by realizing the first interview and for writing a prologue that captured the essence and motivation behind this book. Thank you one more time for being the godmother of yet another one of our projects.

To Sergi Camara, through his photography, for helping the reader to visualize the diffucult journey that most refugees have made to arrive in Greece. To Brad Fredricks for the drone footage.

To all the cooks of Eleonas Camp. Thank you for opening the doors of your homes and of your hearts. Thank you for sharing your culture, recipes and words. Thanks for teaching us that there is always an option, that with strength and bravery everything is possible.

To Selena Herrera, Krista Hochstetler, Lucy Peploe, Rebekah Cheng, Natalia Navarro, Daniela Dini, Brandi Shapland, Emmy Todd, Pablo Rubio and all of the volunteers of Project Elea who participated with enthusiasm in creating the book; doing interviews, tasting amazing recipes and recording the process.

To Simone for putting life into this book with your design. Thank you for the love, patience, perseverance and commitment you put into your work. Without you this wouldn't have been possible.

To the Eleonas community. Thank you for welcoming us, for each cup of tea, for each warm smile, for each 'chetori?', each 'ça va?' and each 'Insha'Allah!'

Fran.

projectelea

Share your experience
#RecipesWelcomeTheBook

Thoughts / Reflections ...

#safepassage
#refugeeswelcome

Made in the USA
Columbia, SC
26 December 2018